Candle Making

How to Instructions, Equipment and Techniques

By: Kaye Dennan

ISBN-13: 978-1492234395

TABLE OF CONTENTS

PUBLISHERS NOTES

Disclaimer

The information presented here is accurate to the best of my knowledge and common candle making practices as of the time of this writing. The author and the publisher accept no liability for the use or misuse of any of the information presented here. This article is presented for informational purposes and is used at your own risk.

Paperback Edition

Manufactured in the United States of America

INTRODUCTION

The Beginners Guide

Are you starting a new and exciting hobby? Or even hoping to start a money-making venture with candle making?

Either way it is a really wonderfully artistic hobby. It is one where you can let your imagination go wild.

I am going to assume you don't know anything about candle making, so with the information here you will have a good basic grounding to start your hobby or money making venture.

Although candle making is relatively easy to do, it is really important to read our *Candle Making Safety* section **before you start** so that you are set up correctly and have the right safety equipment on hand.

EQUIPMENT YOU NEED FOR

CANDLE MAKING

The following are the items you will need to do candle making:

1. Melting Pot
2. Numerical Thermometer
3. Pour Pot
4. Scale to weigh your wax
5. Hammer to break up wax
6. Wire whisk
7. Heat proof gloves and pliers
8. Molds
9. Glue Gun
10. Popsicle sticks

Let me expand on these:

1. MELTING POT
The use of a double boiler is a popular method of melting wax – a little slower but by far the safest. As you get more experience you can look at other methods, but not directly on the stove top until you really know what you are doing and only for certain types of wax.

2. THERMOMETER
You need a good numerical thermometer and you need to use this in conjunction with any type of melting pot.

3. POUR POT
These come in all shapes and sizes but preference should be given to an aluminium "candle makers" pour pot or to a heat proof jug.

4. SCALES
For the hobby candle maker you would probably be starting off with about 4 lbs of wax whilst you are learning. Make sure the scales are nice solid ones not flimsy ones.

5. HAMMER
This is simply used to break the wax up into chunks to be able to weigh it and also put it in the double boiler.

6. WIRE WHISK
Used for blending fragrances and mixing in dyes.

7. GLOVES and PLIERS

Handle ALL hot containers with gloves on or with pliers. Depending on what you are using you may need heat proof gloves or otherwise cotton gloves will do for warm items.

8. MOLDS
Depending on what candles you are going to make you will need to acquire molds.

9. GLUE GUN
For gluing in wick pins on certain molds. Sometimes you can secure the wicks with blue tac.

10. POPSICLE STICKS OR SIMILAR
Popsicle sticks or flat sided pencils are used to hold the wicks in place on certain molds.

SUPPLIES TO MAKE

YOUR CANDLES

Now you are ready to purchase your candle making supplies.

You will need the following supplies:
1. Candle Wax
2. Wax colouring or dye
3. Fragrance Oil
4. Wicks and wick pins

Some more information to help you:

1. CANDLE WAX
You will need candle wax. To start with, you will probably do batches of about 4 lbs at a time. There are many types of wax available and you will need to read up on these depending on the job you want to do. BUT I would suggest even at the beginning don't use cheap and nasty wax because you will think you are doing something wrong when in fact it may only be your choice of wax causing the problem.

2. WAX COLORING AND DYES
Candle wax dyes are easily available and using concentrates they do last a long time and give good color. Not only that, if you use inferior products you may find that the candle does not burn as efficiently as it should.

3. FRAGRANCE OIL

There are many of these on the market and it is only by shopping around and experimenting that you will know what suits your purposes best. Concentrates give the best fragrance and longest fragrance but there are also diluted oils around and you can decide what is best for you. BUT again think this through carefully. If you are going to sell fragrant candles and wish for return sales you should use the best available.

4. WICKS

This is one area that you do have to do some experimentation. You will be looking for a good burn and scent throw. Using different sizes of wick will give a different result. You will also need wick pins to suit. Your supplier should be able to help you with this when you explain the project you are going to do.

Tabbed Wicks

TIPS TO BE AWARE OF FOR BETTER CANDLE MAKING

Work area
Prepare your work area and keep it clean with plenty of room to move around. Make sure all your candle making needs are within reach. **Especially** the chemical fire extinguisher

Preparing the molds
Prepare your molds before you start melting your wax. Make sure they are clean with wicks in place and ready for heating before you pour. Warm molds will prevent you from having 'pour marks' down the side of your molds. If you are having trouble with the candles coming out use a mold release on the inside before pouring.

Glass molds MUST be heated before being poured into. Start with a cold oven and oven heat glassware to approximately 150 degrees before filling with wax.

UV lighting
Check with your supplier about the wax you use because you don't want your candles fading. You may need to add a UV Inhibitor.

Second pour
To prevent a dip in the top of your candles you will need to top up your candles (do a second pour) when your wax in the mold is

cool to touch. Heat the wax (making sure to give it a couple of minutes good stirring) to approximately 10 degrees hotter than your first pour, then top up your candles. If you have left your candles to get cool enough the top should remain nice and flat. But if you do a second pour when the original wax was still too warm the completed candle will have a nipple effect at the top.

It is important that when using colored wax that the second pour is done with some of the original wax or the color may not match.

Wicks

It is possible to buy pre-tabbed and pre-waxed wicks, but it is up to you what you buy. Wicks are a very important part of candle making because of the burn factor. You will need to research this, especially if you are making more novelty candles. You will get plenty of help from a good supplier.

Flat Candle Base

If the base of your candle is not flat simply place it on a hot pan surface and melt it down so that it is flat.

CANDLE MAKING SAFETY

Read These Safety Instructions before You Start Candle Making

For your own safety, the safety of children and the safety of your home it is important that you observe strict safety rules when making candles.

If you do, then you will enjoy your hobby so much more. Not only will it be more enjoyable but accidents will be significantly fewer.

Fire should not be a common problem when observing strict safety rules but you should always be prepared when melting wax.

1.   **Never** leave melting wax unattended. If you have to leave the area **remove the wax off the heat**!

2.   Wax has a flash point ranging between 290 to 380 degrees so **always use a numerical thermometer** in your wax when melting. Know the flash point of any particular wax you are using. If you do not know it, keep the temperature **UNDER 210 degrees. THIS IS VERY IMPORTANT**.

3.   **Always** use a thermometer and keep records (well away from your work area) so you can get repeatable results, especially if you are going to sell your products.

4.   **Do not** melt wax in a pot straight on the element. **Always** use a double boiler whilst you are learning the craft. Heat can be better controlled and in most cases you will be able to heat the wax hot enough to create your candles.

If you are going to use wax requiring a hotter temperature than 200 degrees then you will need to heat the wax directly on the heat. **This needs extra care**. Never go away from the melting wax.

Do not heat the wax over 325 degrees and preferably outdoors for safety reasons.

5.   **Never** have open flames anywhere near wax at any stage – **wax is flammable**. This relates to your work area and to your storage area.

6.   **Fire. Switch off the heat**. Do not attempt to remove the pan.   **Never** put water on a wax fire. Wax is basically an oil. Water and oil don't mix and any water may splatter the wax causing harm.

A MUST! A **chemical** fire extinguisher should be kept near your working area at all times! This is essential for personal safety and the safety of your home.

Keep a pot lid in your working area to extinguish any fire that may occur in the melting pot. Smother flames in the melting pot with a saucepan lid or a damp cloth/towel.

7.   **Handling hot pots and containers**. Always protect your hands when handling hot items. Wear heat resistant gloves or use pliers. Cotton gloves could be used to taking warm containers from the oven.

8.   **Clothing**. Wear loose clothing (and not sheer) so that if the wax splashes it won't touch your skin. Not so loose though that it will catch on things.

9.   **Wax On Your Skin. Immediately** run the area under COLD water and then you can peel off the wax.

10.   **Discarding Unwanted Wax**. Always pour unwanted wax into a metal container and let it set. Never pour wax down the drain as it will set inside the drain and you will need plumbing attention.

TIP. If you pour unwanted wax into a metal container you can cut it into squares before it sets and use these cubes in other candles for variety eg. Pillars or Container Candles, and then top them up with melted wax.

11.   Keep some old newspapers nearby when melting wax as these can be used to clean up any spills.

12.   Not so much a safety tip. To get wax out of clothing or carpets scratch off as much excess wax as you can, then put several layers of paper towel on the area and use a heated iron on the paper to melt the wax and draw it into the paper. Clothing may be dipped in very hot water which will melt the wax.

MAKING YOUR OWN CANDLES

Two Colored Pillar Candle

First off, we will give instructions for making a basic shaped candle in a round pillar mold using two or more colors. Do not be concerned if these candles have imperfections, this is part of the interest of them, but you will experience the basics of candle making. If you don't feel confident using two colors to start, just use one and then go on to using two or more colors at a later date.

For each candle you will need:
Pillar Wax
51-32-18z six inch Wick
Two colours of dye of your choice
Fragrance oil

Kaye Dennan

1   3" x 3.5" round pillar mold
3 inch Wick Pin

Method:
Step 1   Prepare your mold. Insert wick pin through the bottom of the mold. Secure the base of the wick pin to the mold using hot glue. Push pin up tight to the mold and allow too dry. Doing this will keep the wick pin in place.

Step 2   Melt your wax to 170-175 degrees using your thermometer.

Step 3   Add your candle dye. Use only candle dyes for suitable for candle wax. Add your dye slowly (checking for color) and be sure that you stir it for a full 2 minutes using a wire whisk so that the wax and dye blend together.

Step 4   Add your fragrance oil, stirring again for a further 2 minutes to blend fully. **Watch** your temperature and keep it between 170 – 180 degrees when adding your fragrance.

Step 5   To make a multi colored candle you can just layer the colors straight up the candle.

But if you want to achieve a multi-coloured candle with the color angled, you will need to slant your mold and to do this effectively you will need to find something that will hold the mold at an angle safely and securely.

Step 6   Warm your pour pot and you can start pouring your first color.

I would suggest pouring the first color at 170 degrees (you may need to experiment with this – take notes!) **Remember** use your thermometer and keep your wax at all times between 170 – 185 degrees.

Step 7   Let the first color cool until firm, but not pulling away from sides. The mold and wax should still be slightly warm when you pour the second color.

Step 8   Pour the second color at close to 168 degrees and if using only two colors, fill up the mold. It might be that you don't need a second pour of this color, but it is suggested that you poke a relief hole in the top beside the wick (don't pierce the color below) and top up the candle for a flat finish on the top.

Points to note
It is important that the temperature of the second colored wax is cooler than the first lot of wax otherwise the two colours will blend. It is also important that it is not <u>too</u> cool or the layers will not stick together.

Step 9   Allow the candle to harden and then slide from the mold.

Step 10   Clean the molds.

Depending on the number of colors you use as to how many times you will need to angle the mold. This is a great method to play with and come up with some interesting color combinations.

How to Make Votive Candles

These are good "starter" candles.

You will need:
Candle Wax for Votive candles (1 lb makes 8 votives)
Fragrance Oil
Candle Dye
Wicks and Wick Pins
Molds

Method:
Step 1   Melt your wax to 170 – 185 degrees using your thermometer.

Step 2   Prepare your molds with wick pins. Wick pins are not essential with these smaller candles but they do help keep the wicks centred.

Step 3   Add your candle dye. Use only candle dyes for this job. Add your dye slowly (checking for color) and be sure that you stir it for a full 2 minutes using a wire whisk so that the wax and dye blend together.

Step 4   Add your fragrance oil, stirring again for a further 2 minutes to blend fully. **Watch** your temperature and keep it between 170 – 180 degrees when adding your fragrance.

Step 5   Warm your pour pot and you can start pouring your votives. Fill your molds right to the top and let cool. Turn the wax in your boiler down or off. You will use the balance of this wax to top up the molds.

TIP – if using colored wax make sure you keep enough to top up the molds so that you don't have different colors on the top of the candle.

TIP – at the point of pouring note the temperature of the wax.

Step 6 (optional – only if not using wick pins) When a thin skin forms on the top of the wax gently push a wick through to the bottom of the mold. Ensure that this is centred then let the candle set.

Step 7 (optional)   Relief holes can now be made next to the wicks. As votives are so small these are often not made as they are in bigger candles, but if you are going to do this then you do it at this stage.

Step 8 Topping up your candles when your wax in the mold is cool to touch. Heat the wax (making sure to give it a couple of good stirs) to approximately 10 degrees hotter than your first pour, then top up your candles. If you have left your candles to get cool enough the top should remain nice and flat. But if you poured when the original wax was still too warm the completed candle will have a nipple effect at the top.

Step 9 Clean the molds.

Ice Candles

Have you seen these types of candles?
They are one of my favourites.
You can do so much with them.

The idea of these candles is to make really unusual shapes. They can be quite a good way to use up some of your left over colored waxes. You will be using a basic candle making method.

You will need:
Candle Wax
Fragrance Oil (Optional)
Candle Dye
Wicks and/or Wick Pins
Ice cubes or crushed ice
Molds

Method:

Step 1   Decide on your mold – I have seen these made in milk cartons, other types of wax cartons, pyramid shaped molds and many other shapes as well. Set up your wick depending on the type of mold you use.

Step 2 Place ice cubes in your mold. The cubes can be various shapes and sizes. Even crushed ice in larger chunks is good too. The more varied the better.

IMPORTANT – make sure that the area surrounding your wick is free of ice cubes. There needs to be a solid thickness of wax around the wick to ensure a good burn.

Step 3 Melt your wax to 170 – 175 degrees using your thermometer.

Step 4 Add your candle dye. Use only candle dyes for this job. Add your dye slowly (checking for color) and be sure that you stir it for a full 2 minutes using a wire whisk so that the wax and dye blend together.

Step 5   Add your fragrance oil, stirring again for a further 2 minutes to blend fully. **Watch** your temperature and keep it between 170 – 180 degrees when adding your fragrance.

Step 6 Warm your pour pot and slowly pour wax over the ice cubes and build up a solid layer of wax around the wick.

Step 7   You won't need a second pour with this style of candle, unless of course you are using a second color, so just let the ice cubes melt and the wax set hard and release the candle from the mold.

MORE INNOVATIVE CANDLE IDEAS

These can be stunning and sell fantastically
at Party Plans and markets. Probably as much
as anything else because they are all individual.

Embeds

CUBED WAX

Using your excess wax that has been set in trays you can cut these
into cubes and stack them into molds and pour wax around them
to form abstract colored candles. In the picture below you will see
the wax shapes in the solid wax. This technique looks great for
making easy candles as Christmas by using red and green wax
inside solid white wax.

COFFEE BEANS

Add coffee beans to the base of your molds and coffee essence to the wax for the fragrance. Gently pour in the wax. In this particular picture the beans come right to the top and a cylinder of wax has been placed in the center.

SHELL SELECTION

Stack shells into the mold and pour wax around them. Keep shells away from the wick ensuring the wick will have a solid thickness of wax around it for a good burn.

Add Ons

JEWELLERY AND BRIC A BRAC

Beads and other ornaments can be glued to the outside of the candle to adorn it for all occasions. Don't glue anything flammable like lace, near the top of the candle.

You can choose to decorate around the candle, up and down or even crosswise. A glue gun will be sufficient to glue these types of add-ons to your candle.

PICTURES/PETALS/LEAVES

With some clear melted wax you can brush over these items and adhere them to the side of the candle. This is a good way to personalise a candle.

You can choose a fragrance to suit what you are putting on the outside as in the candle below you could use a lavender scent.

GLUING TISSUE PAPER

Another technique which looks great and can be used for a variety of occasions is the covering of candles with tissue paper or the gluing of transfers to the outside.

As you will see in the picture they can look really delicate and suitable for a wedding or they can be quite boisterous with patterns for New Year's Eve and the like.

This technique can also be used to attach photos to candles.

Care needs to be taken when burning candles with paper glued to the outside of candles.

Hand Painted

You can also personalize candles by painting the outside of the candle by hand. Raised dimensional glues look great as well, especially for Christmas when you can use the dimensional glitter glue.

Molds

SILICONE MOLDS

On the market now you can purchase silicone molds in all shapes for cake making and these molds are also great for candle making. You can either make them as a single color candle or you can pour a little of one color in the mold then add a second color to make a two color piece, for example, that idea looks lovely with a rose flower mold.

COOKIE CUTTERS

Blue tac metal cookie cutters to a firm base and fill with wax. Using the same shape, but in different sizes you can stack these up in different colors.

Cookie cutters can also be used when you spread a slab of melted wax on a paper sheet inside a baking tray. While the wax is still relatively soft cut out shapes and push a wick through from the bottom.

THESE ARE JUST A FEW IDEAS FOR VARIATION
AND THERE LOTS MORE AS
I AM SURE YOU WILL DISCOVER

ENJOY AND HAVE A BUNDLE OF FUN

ABOUT THE AUTHOR

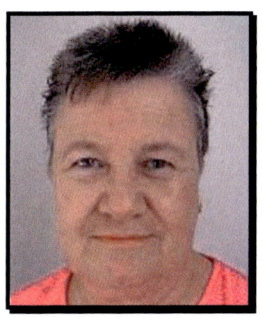

Kaye Dennan has had over 5 years in the arts and crafts field as an instructor and business owner. Kaye has really enjoyed working with wax because of the fact that it is so pliable and is so easily scented and colored.

With this knowledge Kaye decided she wanted to share her enjoyment of the craft and so hence the book **"Candle Making – How To Instructions, Equipment and Techniques"**.

Kaye has also written other books on candle making which may interest you.

---Now Released---

"Candle Making Business – *A Book on How to Start and Run Your Own*"

Made in the USA
Coppell, TX
15 November 2023

24250937R10021